A Long Time Coming
Selected Poetry and Prose

FRED BENTLEY

PAGE PUBLISHING
Conneaut Lake, PA

First originally published by Page Publishing 2024

ISBN 979-8-89315-133-6 (pbk)
ISBN 979-8-89315-146-6 (digital)

Printed in the United States of America

To Tara and Suzanne

With All My Love

Contents

Poetry and Prose

Turning of the Screw

You start again
inevitably
trying to say something
put something together
from some inner passion
for self-expression
and it seems if there
could just be a complete
and total release of this passion
you would grow in bounds
and needing badly to grow
you work at it
and see that element in you
that holds you back
and prevents the growth
from occurring
and yes, you cry out
about social injustice
and insanity and ignorance
you rail against society as
though it could deliver you
and you sit sulking in the deep morass
and you remember that part of you
that could be improved
and made better
and you thirst for it
to fulfill that need for growth
and you must do it as a person
as an individual pursuit that cannot
help but become socialized
because it will thrust you down the path
toward success in your endeavors.

The Time Is Now

You decide to go for it
and it comes upon you
steadily!

You firm up your resolve
to order the act
no time for doubt
or careless thinking!

All that you know must be summoned
and it is a test of how well you
have listened and learned!

It requires a certain single-mindedness
and the highest level of endeavor!

Never mind the fleeting past of the
decadent symbols and bleached indulgences!

SEIZE THIS TIME!

It passes with such
great promise!

SEIZE THIS MOMENT!

It passes quickly
like the summer breeze
you decide to go for it
now do it!

The Way

Riding the township road
grinding the gravel into dust
into snow
into mud
into dust again
taking inventory
examining the land
reading mailboxes and trying to remember
while fighting the sun and the night
learning and teaching
lucidly, eagerly, impatiently, wearily
weaving along the dialectic
turning the contradictions and thinking
and changing and struggling with
social relations and bourgeois organizations
dissecting the class struggle
practicing the only way we know how
and wanting only one thing
A way
struggling for a way
and seeing a way
we make our way!

Seeing the way and understanding the means
and moving forward, critically and dialectically
into a symphony of bright flowers and sunlight
cast against gray shadows
and feeling history at a turning point
and wanting to grasp it and direct it
We shall challenge our very lives!

It is happening
and it has always been happening
and it is powerful
We must tune in to its drumming!

For us, it is a beginning
a single step along the way
to a new beginning
which never ends!

We must mark the days one at a time
with purpose and clarity
and the beginnings shall never cease
to sprout anew!

Struggle

We struggle every day
we all do, and it burns the air we breathe

We struggle with ourselves
to unwind the web that enmeshes our lives

We struggle with the awareness
that it must involve everyone, and until that time
we must struggle for accurate answers
to thrust us further along the road of our endeavors

We don't always succeed
we make many mistakes
and turn many ways along the road

Theory must guide us
taken from the bed of practice
and tested by the fire of living

We enter struggle
with knowledge of the past
and a vision for the future

Unflaggingly, we must struggle
and test the deepest water
churn through the stiffest current
finding strength in the effort
and renewal in the experience

Struggle, Practice, Struggle

Comes the evening and the fire
time passes in the mind and illuminates the present
shapes the future and drives relentlessly

Struggle, Tactics, Resolve
fit together like a coitus
with fervent thought

Practice, Theory, Practice
grow like a tree
rise with the wind and shadow the night

Autumn comes running with subtle force
bringing change, always change
Yes!

Days passing with seasons
growing into years
fearless years aching with clarity and power

Seize it with somber care
nursed by thought and action!
Yes!

Night ebbs into dawn
into autumn
into change drawn from freshness
and galloping into the sun with eager avowals

Yes!

Practice
Struggle
Practice

Yes!

August

Comes August
with the heat of July
with foment and strident dissatisfaction
leaning into the future
conscious of oblivion
entwined in the struggle
engulfed with desire.

Comes August
like the first one
coiled in the womb
seeking deliverance
fermenting with discontent.

Comes August
with ageless inner war
clashing with thoughts
and ideas
laced with emotions.

Comes August
with pinched struggle
sharply honed in ceaseless combat
fueled by need of the highest order.

Comes August
in deep national crises
while the candidates kiss asses
in the political vacuum
that sweeps across our land
like waves crashing upon the shore.

Comes August
and our people suffocate
from lack of jobs
inadequate health care
poor diet
double-digit inflation
undeveloped mass transit
and a badly deteriorating economy.

Comes August
with the shrill cadence of the KKK
and the beating drums of the militaristic right
seeking to reassert global domination.

Comes August
in a maze of brilliant colors
of cascading light
and here we stand!

The Waning of an Epoch

The epochal struggle rages furiously
out of control.

The next quantum leap of people surges forth
poised to explode.

A new order stretches
in awkward but certain birth.

The lure of fabled destiny lives in ruins
within the foul air of environmental plunder.

The Motherland writhes from broken vows
beneath the weight of a crippled industrial machine
while the gilded nobles leave their homes
in a Homerian quest for ancient shores.

Sam rises like a leviathan
stumbling along a narrow path
crushing everything that interferes.

Capitalist kingpins spin the cherished line
but charlatan mouths of hope lose their way
in a dizzy circular fall.

The new gentry is unconcerned
with greedy accumulation
of plastic overconsumption.

The agrarian heritage is smashed
as the old landlords fade away

grinding the rural hierarchy
stubbornly into dust.

The social fabric unravels before our eyes
while the unborn are running out of time.

There is no rejoicing on main street.

Blindman's Bluff

Rich man, poor man
blindman's bluff
when will the rich man have enough?

Rich man, poor man
look across the fields
one sees labor
one sees yields.

Rich man, poor man
both have dreams
but one man screams
while one man schemes.

Rich man dresses with great care
wondering what clothes to wear
poor man futilely gasps for air
caught within the rich man's lair.

Rich man crows with all his might
wouldn't give a nickel for the poor man's plight
poor man struggles with his lot
works with his woman for the little they have got.

Never has there been a land
so full with natural wealth
stop a minute though
and feel the nation's health
it reeks with burning fever
from the rotten swelling greed
the eyes well with pregnant tears
of abandoned social need

the mouth foams with banter
and words of hollow phrase
the heart throbs with wanton lust
a million untold ways.

The doctor says that things are fine
he marvels at our class
while always proclaiming
that the symptoms shall soon pass
but every time the day has come
when the health is supposedly restored
we find the sutures failing
and the wounds agape retorn.

There is a cure for this disease
if only we could see
it's called an equal sharing
among all humanity.

The Cow Jumped over the Moon

no hope
no hope
when mothers die of swollen, burning, upturned breasts

no hope
when newborn babes die of runny, creamy shit

no hope
with hillsides lined with stinking bodies
crawling with gooey maggots

no hope
when crying souls live on in nothingness

no hope
when yesterday's only food comes up in a torrent
and splatters the rat-infested hall

no hope
when the true believer doesn't believe in you

no hope
when the phantom isle is sought and
the rights of man are strangled

no hope
when the dreams of mankind are made impossible
and jeeringly sneered at

no hope
when everything lies just beyond the mined field
and next to the hanging tree

no hope
when love is not really anything but a four-lettered word

no hope
when faith is placed unswervingly in a nonexistent God

no hope
when friends say they are but aren't

no hope for the young, though they be strong

no hope for the old, though they be wise

no hope for the believers for there is nothing to believe in

no hope
no hope at all

The American Poet

The baneful dirges flail into the wind
and beat upon the hollow cavity of the night
with painful self-awareness circling in endless
contradictions seeking truth and forgiveness
tortured by the capitalist noose and sullen
masochism die each brutal night
mindful of the capitalists' murder, plunder, and conquest
yet timid wrapped securely in self.

Awaken American Poet!

You are the great hope of a nation slumbering
in self-possessed stupidity!

You are the fire of dreams that suffocate
within the belly of the beast!

Learn American Poet!

From the clear-mindedness of the Third World
spokesmen who speak in words so clear and plain
that even the conniving imperialist trembles in fear!

Come American Poet!

Let us learn from our native-born
who have suffered and still suffer untold horrors
from the hands of the capitalist jingoes!

Let us speak of the people's history
buried in slavery beneath the lies of the bourgeoisie!

Come!

We have work to do!

The voice of the People must be heard!

Imperialism

The American capitalist imperializes the American people
    exploits our labor
    to extract obscene profits
    to put into their private bank accounts
    and luxurious mansions in the hills
    to flaunt their wealth while
    the people struggle to make ends meet.

Why don't we make them earn their
    own living for a change?

Why do we let them get away with it?

They came upon the land
    the land stolen
    by murder and plunder
    by tricks and empty promises
    devouring the resources
    like a vulture for a pittance
    using the people's labor
    to further their selfish needs
    to pollute the air and water
    to construct wasteful objects
    which they force into our lives
    while they leave the land barren
    and the people destitute.

They come in the name of the State
    and take our hard-earned savings
    to build armaments and make war
    to murder people and make bribes
    and commit heinous crimes to subvert governments

and destroy dreams to terrorize
    and we let them do it.

They come with their power and their greed
    because we let them have it.

Why?

They come into our homes each day
    with lies and treachery
    with their self-serving analysis
    with their celebrations
    with their tragedies
    and we accept it meekly.

They didn't tell us about Wounded Knee
    or Sand Creek
    or Rosewood
    or Haymarket Square.

Just as they didn't tell us about Big Bill Haywood
    and Denmark Vesey
    and Fred Hampton
    and Albert Parsons
    and Joe Hill
    and the multitude of other American patriots
    past and present
    who were crushed beneath the iron heel
    of the capitalist.

The people are powerful
    if we will only accept that power
    and use it for ourselves.

Why don't we do it?

Allende Lives

Allende died today
I don't want to believe it.
A decent man who dared face the reality of tomorrow
and lead his people there…dead.
A strong man with honest dreams…dead.
A resolute man with admirable convictions…dead.
A strong man elected fairly
to free his people from the shackled past
to shape their destiny
to explore their future
to utilize their resources
to build and construct a society worthy of anyone's respect!

But Sam wouldn't hear of it
and Sam gets his way
with his arsenal of putrid self-righteousness
and greed and power and lust
to rule the whole damn world!

Allende died today.
Sam killed him.
Sam of a thousand faces
who rapes the earth for fun and profit
who sticks his dagger in the belly of the world
who swells with rotten wealth
and wouldn't think of sharing it
who claims to lead the fight for freedom
but who knows not the freshness of the word
who bullies small people and smiles
and hides behind the corporate skirt
preaching self-determination
fighting wars and

killing sons
in his vengeful, hypocritic, fanatic wrath!

Allende died today
but not in vain
for Sam will die of his own hand
and Allende will live!

The Pottawatomie Power Plant Blues

Gather around
    there's a story I have to tell
    about the farmers' struggle
    with the KP&L.

One fine day, in the spring of '73
a power plant was planned
the biggest you'll ever see.

In the land of the Pottawatomie
    where the wildlife once did roam
    where the wind and flowers blew free
    and the brave Indians made their home.

Near Belvue
where the bluegrass grew tall
they came and told the farmers
they'd have to move by fall.

Bal Jeffery sent out his man
so full of greed and gall
but he was met by angry men
who weren't afraid to stall.

They took their rights to court
where they hoped the judge would spare
the unknown future dangers
and the loveliness of clean air.

Well
    Judge Brookens didn't see it that way
    he said the company was within their rights
    as clear as any day.

And the people did excitedly exclaim
we'll run short some time
and I don't want to be the blame.

So the land was changed
to conform with future use
and soon the smokestacks rose
and ruined the air with no excuse.

The acid rain did scatter across the land
till the native grasses wilted
and the crops couldn't even stand.

The people
    they grew nervous
    when they looked into the sky
    they saw the grimy haze
    and couldn't even remember why.

The Game Groveller

The hand, the soil, the sea
the reticulation of the continual harmony
and conflict of each into the other
into the ultimate accumulated million laboring
sounds of the earth's rolling vastness.

Found without seeking
joined without asking
endured without culminating.

The game groveller
inclined toward reticence
mindful of his father's heart
seeks without finding
lives beyond all knowledge
a stranger to himself.

Time passes like a dream
evanescent with great weariness
but lasting, always like a shadow, never fading.

And passing, thus, does the groveller live
immersed in contradictions
alienated against himself
deprived of the realization of the greatest dream
the enjoyment and benefit of his own labor
molded into being by the dictates of his surroundings
cast into life to fill the needs of others
striving within a swirling cloud
that fogs the mind and thwarts the will.

And so
he finds himself cowering before the throne
a stranger still within the paled rainbow of stifled being
weeping tears of blood
delivered into eternal trysting.

Aghast, he asks for deliverance but is denied.
Desperately, he begs for forgiveness but is shunned aside.
With halting breath, he seeks re-creation but finds only oblivion.

At last he turns unto the Mother
and takes her open hand
and sees for the first time
her great plan of dialectical reasoning
weaving and threading its way through history.

He feels the fetters loosen
and new life flows easily through his tortured being.

Thus, does he begin anew
whole and dignified
discarding slowly the molded life
and feeling the great dream softly rumbling.

Who Am I

Who am I
in this world of greed and righteous plunder
where nations reel with rampant hunger.

Who am I
in these times of trouble and world disorder
where violence rules in every quarter.

Who am I
beneath the morning sun and cool air
where meadowlarks sing and fools stare.

Who am I
along the streets, I walk and ask
as beggars plead behind their masks.

Who am I
when the rain pours down in the afternoon
and the clouds are dark with impending doom.

Who am I
huddled in the storm with internal strife
seeking relief from this maddening life.

Who am I
as the darkness falls with a pale moon
looking for a friend within my gloom

Who am I
to count the stars in the calming night
when a fresh wind blows with all its might.

Who am I
to right the wrongs of many a year
when darkness clings beside my fear.

Who am I
in the early dawn pf sleeplessness
with futile thoughts of her caress.

Who am I
it never ceases its constant roar
reaching out to give me more.

Who am I
to right the wrongs of many a year
when darkness clings beside my fear.

I Dance Alone

In the dimly studded diamond night
the music sobs a mellow tone
the baffled sounds around me cling
echoes of the words I sing
within my ear the solid drone
I move my feet
I dance alone.

Looking at the world, I stare
feeling frigid to the bone
the music seeps across the room
an empty space of gloom and doom
around my head the reeking moan
I crank it up
I dance alone.

When justice fails across the globe
and harmony away has flown
it seems not right
to feel the fright
of selfish grief so overblown
I bow my head
I dance alone.

Across the land, a shadow grows
amidst the greed that people hone
the child cries and wisdom dies
the sorrowful sound of patience sighs
the seed of death has been sown
I shake my fist
I dance alone.

Within my heart a fatal burst
a loss of hope I used to own
love begone into sadness
anger turned to madness
I close my eyes
I dance alone.

The End of Summer

Late August wind crashes through the boughs
beneath the glow of the full orange moon
Vividly come the changes with sweeping certainty
captured within the sounds of night
The night reaches out with giving
and yields its flowing

Blue eyes passing in the night
Passing, passing
seeing change weaving in a narrowing spiral
entering the currents of being
The aspects of change collide
in triangular screenings
and casts the being onward
with aching avowals

The wind rises and falls rhythmically
and drives time into its current
and the movement quickens
through the August maze
so unusually bright with
springlike brilliance

Eyes meeting in the night of time
seeking deliverance
knowing of the change and
mindful of the uncertainties
pass in the night

Rain comes with the wind
August rain
and the current freshens
with flowing certainty
It is now and it is always
and always will be
It comes and exerts control
and divides and flourishes with reunion
It guides the current and the current responds
and always responds and hastens from where it has been

August time slipping into autumn
gathering speed from within gathered speed
pushing time pushing the current
with trebled force relentlessly
and hastening
the current divides
within the stream and placid water dwells
upon the bank with ripples toward the sea

Ripples waving grow from one to many
and back to one again with harmonious striving
only to be thrust into the current
speeding with certainty toward the inevitable
oneness of the sea
and the being flows with it
out of oneness seeking oneness
once again

Blue eyes waiting in the change
peering out at change
marvelous change
Blue eyes seeking and receiving
and driving into the night
August night of tempest clashing
of reasoned fantasy

of stubborn living
of oneness seeking oneness
begging for practice
and finding the Mother's
great yielding.

The Way I Feel

Echoes of a voice I hear
Memories of the past I fear
Stifled dreams within the clouds
Destruction reigns atop my crown

Darkness knocks at passion's door
Falls apart upon the floor
The futile efforts of my resolve
Gather force and then dissolve

Oh, Mama
The way I feel!

Flowers bloom in the afternoon
Casts a shadow on my gloom
Love is gone, will not return
The life I sought has been spurned

Happiness ends before it begins
My focus dulls behind the lens
Chaos grinds into the night
Leaves me blinded without sight

Oh, Mama
The way I feel!

There is nothing left to fight for
Nothing left to win
The curious path to freedom
Is dusty now and grim

Life is such a torrent
Life is such a dream
Laden with this feeling
I can't even scream

Oh, Mama
The way I feel!

The wind is off the sail
The rudder is in the ground
The waves are rolling backward
And I can't hear a sound

The glow is off the polish
Red is off the rose
The midnight song a serenade
Of words I can't disclose

Oh, Mama
The way I feel!
But, Mama, my sweet Mama
Don't you fret for me
Life is not what it seems to be
Right is left, and left is right
War is peace, and peace is strife
Who knows what the eye can see

Oh, Mama
I just want to be free!

The Granite Night

Madness in the granite night
Paupers pawn to pimp's delight
Prostitutes fawn at every door
Upholding pillars of capitalist war
Righteous malevolence patrols the run
Cleaning nails with the handle of a gun
Epicurean feasts of ruin foredoom
Falling shadows of hedonist gloom
Lancers feel of razor-thin skill
Elucidate clearly the field of kill
Towers of Babel built upon the sea
Swarm the mass of never met to be
Planners' play is glutted to the core
Another pillar of capitalist war
Alien's paradise knifes away the fruit
Tolerance rots into the Mother's roots
Think not a thought of the damnable waste
Seeping from the sockets of incompetent haste
Stifled in the trumpets of the unblown horn
Wretched in the dying and the unknown born
Burnt in the alley of the junkies ripped arm
Crafted in the pillage of a foreign farm
Madness rules the granite night
Pillared wildly with capitalist might

The Dark Earth

There is a sadness in the world today
that bring tears to my burning eyes.

It is for humanity that I cry
the lost ideals
the tortured spirit
of wise men scorned.

The illuminated light of love gone dark.
The blissful embrace of brotherhood blown asunder.
The needed touch of understanding lost.
To the rampant roar of armies.

The crescent-shaped moon from above
views the disgrace of nations glorified in blood
the blood of common people
taunted in their daily quests.

Mournful sounds of death haunt the dark earth
raped by greed
searching for glory in honor's sake.

The lonely surf pounds the shore
warning in the beacon light
the betrayal of human goodness.

There is a sadness in the world today
that is madness!

The Hole in the Head Man

The hole in the head man was a sight to see
you could look through his head so perfectly
what you saw in there was a failure to grow hair
but you couldn't get him to release it

Now you or me or all of humanity
could easily tell that this man wasn't well
but you couldn't get him to admit it

He ran up the hill, carrying a glass with a pill
when he got to the top, he looked back at the drop
and couldn't imagine how he got there

This fool on the hill with his pieces of eight
counted his change and ignored his fate
his mind was so empty and devoid of a soul
that sleighloads of reindeer could dance through his hole

His lack of a mind was curious enough
he lost it one day below a white bluff
he was young at the time and thought little of it
until he was older and needed a hit

There was no time then to think of the loss
with all of the clamor of life's brittle gloss
he ranted and raved at all pretty things
until he was lost in the delusion it brings

Enticed out of madness, he championed the hill
and wound up there one day with a glass and a pill

Now the hole in the head guy never wondered why
he just looked through his legs to the sky
he bent over so far, he dropped his glass jar
and shattered it to pieces

Frantically, he searched for his little white pill
but his efforts were futile, for it had fallen down the hill
left all alone without any help
the wind roared a fury so bad it caused welts

He realized too late that the hill had been a bait
sent there by life's sultry trappings
left alone, now his life finished unwrapping

The Blasphemy

We've come this far with fascination
We've come this far with grief
We've come this far to realization
We've come this far to weep.

It's been sometimes inspirational
It's been cruel and harsh
It's been sometimes stupefying
It's been a real farce.

I wonder if it's always been like this
I would imagine that it has
Too bad the weapon wasn't nourished
Too bad the general wasn't had.

The neon lights are always dazzling
The neon lights are always bright
The neon lights are self-defying
They are bored and skewered of blight.

What a wasteful incantation
What a wasteful lark
What a futile aberration
What a futile way to start.

What a boring acclimation
What a boring sight
We've seen the real believers
We've seen them living right.

A blasphemy of total living
A blasphemy of total life
A travesty of wholesomeness
A travesty of bitter strife.

Truth has a way of fleeing
When the flames of passion rise
Freedom echoes in a hollow air
Trapped in the cataclysmic lair.

We've come this far with resignation
We've come this far with dreams
We've come this far to battle
Against the power structure's schemes.

An Old Feeling

I'm starting out colder
than I've ever been
I let that damn feeling
get me again
and it's getting harder
with every step that I take
the hours and the days
and the time that I waste
but if you could teach me
I wish that you would
I can't stand this feeling
any more than you could.

I've got a life
so fine and so true
filled with so much desire
it makes me feel blue
so I've got learning
to take in my stride
and I must have changes
left in my ride
but if you think it's easy
let me tell you some more
my bags are sitting
packed by the door.

I've sought out the answers
as well as I can
and considered my options
and my life as a man
with thought of this life
and where I must stand

and given the future
a most careful scan
and decided the ways
that I won't be bought
the causes to chase
and the ends to be sought
but if you think it's easy
let me tell you one thing
I've let that old feeling
hit my head with a ring.

I came filled with searching
for a way I could be
I think it was wanting
to feel I was free
but somehow my searching
has not given me
that feeling of freedom
I wanted to see.

A Fading Crown of Leaves

A red-ember fire glows before me
as ecstatic visions of life dance through my mind:

    a crowded city street with neon lights flashing
    an old building enamored with rusty railings and filthy walls
    a river bridge bustling with heavy traffic
    a mountain stream guiding sparkling, clean water around gray
        boulders
    a springtime rain glistening brilliantly in the heavily ladened grass
    a brown-furrowed field stretching across the flatlands
    potato-shaped hills set against a brooding sky
    a fresh smile on a dim day
    bare skin melting before the sun.

Each giving reasons to hope
    a way of living
    an end in itself
    never self-sustaining
    only lasting for a moment
    always just a moment.

Is there no more
than this fleeting glimpse of wonder
which echoes into a shattering night?

I fall headlong into the abyss
grasping futilely at the darkness
failing to perceive the pigmentation of my own skin.

What desperate demon has scorched my soul
and thrust it into chaos?

I have not had to prove myself
or walked down mirrored halls
or pass before the reviewing stand
to receive the plaudits
yet I have desired it.

I have seen the truth
and shrunk back
seeking the image of time
lost forever
a soliloquy
of never was and never will be.

The wings of indignant hysteria
powered by the awesome strength of the wind
thrusts me to the heavens
and shoots out endlessly into space.

Who could say it better
than the streetcar conductor
who told me to get off
when I arrived at where
I didn't know I always wanted to be.

Interlude

A match strikes
burns into the night
and dies

Winter sky gleams
and falls away

Time slows
running nowness
to a halt
tempting passion
to a burst
but holding inside
the presence
of incredible choices
so infinite in their range

And then
control divides
cascades the night
with flames
of competing might
causing strife to wade
through the mountaintops

And the east wind meets
the west wind and swirls
around the earth
comingled

Around blows the wind
without ceasing
always returning
to the place it has been
and time remains forever
steadily beating

The moon grows
into middle January
marked by mild days
and crisp nights

The earth rolls
and the Big Dipper
stands on its handle
with an empty cup

The days bring a
certain air of change
with a definite turn
in the making

The nights creep by with
a slight easing of intensity
relaxed by thoughtful reflection
and reasoned purpose
coexisting with the old
in temporary peace

Thus, does January slip by with
the key turning in the lock

A dog barks endlessly
into chiseled night
an owl hoots its wisdom low

frogs croak dryly
crickets creak

Trains rumble past leaving
a hollow ring in the
unyielding night
a soft breeze hisses
through the screen
a window rattles back
a leaky faucet drips…drips…
floors squeak beneath the
tireless, ageless feet of ghosts
and you wait patiently
for the great healer
the blessed sleep
and the world waits with you
and waiting waits

Time to get a move on
time to get going
time to turn the screw
into the wheel
time to dig the
shovel into the earth
time to press motives
time to take a step
like the wind that comes
before the rain
bringing seasonal chill
time to get ready
for all that is to come

Waiting for the Sun

Sunrise on an autumn day
she stood there like a rose
early light descended
with golden rays upon her head
bursting pearls of warmth cascaded
moist against her skin
Phaethon rose above the earth
powerful with his reins
he stood there like a warrior
crimson with the day

Over the mountaintop
a delicate shadow cast
bathing her with soothing light
radiant with its glow
grooves of the earth lay before me
trampled with human passing
the roads seemed to lead anywhere
I would want to go
and I felt like a mountain
and she the sun

Wind exhaled
blew from every way
and settled in the east
her coming christened me
with yearning, aching like
a roaring tumult
from every corner of the land

With spangled beauty before me
golden haze upon her hair

she seemed so close to touch
softly flowing was her warmth
so fair and delicately soothing
bonding gentle breath with lovely song
upon the earth as birds and wind
will do

I felt a certain quiver
as Phaethon struggled with his mounts
it surged within my bones
and rose unbound with passion
beside her perfect pose
carpet sky of blueness
blending clouds with stretching sea
of waving life and rolling earth
of brilliant light upon the fields
and there I stood the mountain
and she the sun

Yellow day of browning earth
reaping bounty by the hand
she grew into me
burning boldly with seasons turning
into days
approaching night
she blazed there with my future

Blinded by Phaethon's plight
I thought the earth would fly away
haste of day into cool night
of horizon ringed with fire
and wind hastening to a
a feeling of fresh loneliness
believing in the dawn
and I the mountain
she the sun

Mississippi-Bound

I'm Mississippi-bound, my friends
I'm Mississippi-bound
to where the broad Minnesota plains
meet the rolling Wisconsin Dells.

I'll ride up Dylan's highway
to the north country fair
and take the ride back upon the Delta Queen
past the old wayfarer's inn
where trappers used to stay.

I'll ride among the coolies
and seek the virgin pine
where tall siloes rise
behind the great red barns.

I'm Mississippi-bound, my friends
I'm Mississippi-bound
where the ducks stay north in winter
in the icy wonderland
where the muskrats build their lodges
where Goose Island hides that snow-white fawn.

I'll bed beside the river
and feel that Mississippi mud
and lay my head to rest
with ears for tug boats
chugging for the locks.

I'm Mississippi-bound, my friends
I'm Mississippi-bound
where oil burns the night with history's pungent fumes

where Marquette and Joliette bared
the frigid, hard winter.
I can see them now on a grim tundra day
looking for the indigenous born
to change from savage ways.

I'm Mississippi-bound, my friends
I'm Mississippi-bound
I'll watch ol' Joel the mountain man
split a log with a single blow
and sit beside his hearth and
feel the embers glow
and when it's time to sleep
I'll lie with Dylan in the air
and think about my past
but the parting won't be easy
and my tracks will be well-kept
I'll be thinking Mississippi
all the way back west.

Pieces of Dreams

When the corn rows flicker by like spinning wheels
and the white lines streak past like shooting stars
the road becomes narrow and stretches on forever.

Heat waves ripple at the edge of the earth
and somnolent tiptoe steps graze the treetops
a soft cushion for the hard ride.

Fly with soaring wings
into time
out of time
lost in time
like a wandering stead, floating by in the moonlight
casting the elusive shadow of its image on the desert floor
and the rain that falls on the windswept western plains as
streaks of red on the gray horizon gather forth the dawn.

Scattered fragments of broken promises and
yesterday's memories create a fantasy
of possible alternatives that linger
and fade into the spinning wheel
sliding smoothly, like a million freshly oiled tumblers.

Ride the spinning wheel and listen
the plaintive cry of a lost soul beckons.

Rebirth

Bright moonlight in the cool morning air
unruffled in its nocturnal peace
beckoned me from my bed with a mesmeric tug.
The cosmic rays glided over my graceful cantor
into the tall grass, wet with not yet glistening dew.
I rode the mystical union along the edges
of a gently flowing brook flourishing
with musical sounds of nightlife still alive.

At the junction of a larger stream
I danced across the rocks
dampening my toes in the frigid wake
and climbed a bank to prop against a towering pine.
Gathering my breath in rapid bursts
I sat in awe of nature
to be a raindrop and merge with others
to flow to the sea
to be a swell of wind cascading over the land
or a crust of soil dislodged from the earth
to be deposited in far-off places.

This was my desire and yearning.
Coming close to living is being near rebirth
and blessed with wings of immortality
I willed it and became.

The Free Spirit

Wild and free
      the untamed
    like the fire and the passion
of the wind.
     The stretching prairie
       pure and clean
          always.
Excursions of the mind
      lapses into time
    the rhythms of other worlds
        beating in the mind.

The Country

If I could tear myself away
from this sniveling rat pack world
I'd return to the country of rolling hills
with miles upon miles of open space
that gradually meet the sky.

I'd live on one of those hills
just above a gently flowing stream
encased by rocks and shale
its banks outlined by tall cottonwoods
and spreading willows.

In the mornings, I'd be up at dawn
to usher in the new day
to watch the early morning dew
glisten in the first rays of the sun.

I'd romp undisturbed in green pastures
with full energy and delight
not stopping until I could go no further.

Time would be nothing more than freedom
with the sun at its peak for the day and
beside the sparkling stream beneath the shade
I'd dangle my toes in the only visible
remnants of the winter snow.

I'd watch nature stake its claim on yet
another year and give hearty support
to all the little things in its constant struggle.

My time would be spent thinking and sensing
and realizing what it's like to take a
deep exhilarating breath of unpolluted air
to smell the freshness of spring flowers
to hear the peaceful, steady ripples
of my friend, the stream.

At night, I'd linger before sleep
and listen to the lonely croaks of
the frogs down by the stream
to the mosquitoes as they buzz
around their prey
to the howls of the coyotes
searching for friends
and as these sounds filled me
the cool night air sifting ever so
gently through the window screen
it would guide me into pleasant
satisfying slumber.

If I could pull myself away.

The Kingdom

Carl took us out to a place in the pasture
    where he fed the cows in winter
and we took turns steering while he emptied
    sacks of ground grain on the snow
white ground in piles and the cows lined up
    in long rows nibbling at the feed.

The frisky calves did frolic in the lushy
        cream of winter
and their furry hides did glisten in the
        early glow of sunlight
and Carl caught one for us and held him to
        our hands.

The frightened little roan-face shivered in
        our grasp
and let loose a mighty bawl that resounded
        through the pasture
and when at last he kicked free, he went
        streaking for his mother.

Carl chuckled softly, and his eyes danced with
        laughter
and I watched his breath carry in the stubborn
        still of the morning
and the snowbirds singing were a melody of mirth.

I could feel the princes smiling and the power
    of the paupers and the spring flowers
        blooming 'neath the bed of
        pearls of rivers.

We left the jeweled pasture when morn ceased to shimmer
and the golden haze and chastity of magic
spirited us toward home.

A Beckoning Toward Eternity

If you feel that you're dying before it's time
come to my place, and I'll show you what's mine
sit at my table of midsummer fruits
drink from my well, deep in the earth's roots
stand on my floors of oak and white pine
look at my walls, papered with flowers, so fine

Gaze out my front window into the world
see those people with themselves unfurled
what can you see when you look at them
be careful how you judge and how you condemn
they're not much different than you or me
just looking for a home and some liberty

Come out to my garden of vines and rich soil
I'll tell you of long hours burdened by toil
smell the sweet flowers and the blue grass dew
think of what life can mean for you

Stay in my home all through the night
listen to the wind tremble with glorious might
the rustling of leaves, such a gentle delight
sleep the night well and think nothing of fright

Tell me your heartaches, and I'll share with you mine
don't think of dying; we have plenty of time

The Fields of Home

I saw the hills before me
    majestic in their glow
bearing flowers of wildness
    with the wind in gentle tow.

The green grasses were sparkling
    in the early warmth of spring
there was the sound of laughter
    in every living thing.

The birds were singing melodies
    in the freshness of the air
I felt blessed with happiness
    at simply being there.

The land was there before me
    rich with sandy loam
I gazed across the prairie
    and saw the fields of home.

Tryst

Suddenly, she comes to you
she knows you are there
and wants you to know
without you knowing

You want her to want you there
but know she doesn't know
with wants entwined, you have her there
and now she wants to let you know
and when you know
you let her know
and then you both know
what the other knows
and life is succored within the room

What the other has, you both now have
and you pass it back and forth
you trade your wants and trade your knows
and you both know what the other knows
and back and forth
you pass it back and forth
the other to the fore
and wants collide with knows
and knows enmesh with wants
until the succored life is enmeshed no more

She comes to you and runs to you
and you to her without you knowing
and knowing that
you let her know
and when she knows, you pass it back and forth
and she knows she came to you when you were knowing

and wanting her to want you
and know you as you wanted her
and you pass it back and forth
the fore to her
and back to you, and you both know
all there is to know
and the knowing stops

It ends too soon
she has to leave before she knows you know
and knowing that you pass it back and forth
and you know each other again for the short last time
and then the knowing stops
and strangers you are again.

The Calling

Out upon the terra firma
far away from the sea
on heavenly wings
the meadowlark sings
and the bugler summons me.

For what is this time
so fast now running
a puzzling stare
the mental error
truth comes naturally.

For what do we seek
in this moment of our lives
the sudden dare
without a care
and the wind crashes
through the apple tree.

How do we choose
from cross-webbed security
a foolproof lair
of common ware
and the band plays relentlessly.

Where do we go
when all rivers run to the sea
the chance is rare
to pay the fare
and hope springs eternally.

How long do we wait
with all the seasons changing
the time is here
within the fear
and all the rhythms drum quickly.

Out upon the terra firma
far away from the sea
the trumpets blare
in the morning air
and the prairie wind calls
for you and me.

The Stubborn Struggle

The terror
the fear
the self-imposed restraints
that prevent it from igniting
the mental embrace
of emotional delight
smothering it with protection
in a cold, cold night.

The joy
the ecstasy
the oral addiction
against the advice
of the other self
festooned against the night
like a wet leaf on a car hood.

A deadening sound
the swirl of time
a listless groping
on the hardwood floors
separation of self from self
the merging of opposites
clarity and confusion intertwined.

Cold burrows in the January night
the weak resolve
the useless thinking
the frayed fantasy
the unspeakable words
enveloped with mind and body
and the faint glimmer of hope!

Just Thinking

Thinking about love
Thinking about sex
Thinking about survival
in the darkness of the night.

Thinking about war
Thinking about peace
Thinking about the history
of might makes right.

Thinking about life
Thinking about death
Thinking about the struggle
of the eternal fight.

Thinking about good
Thinking about evil
Thinking about the two
entwined within our sight.

Thinking about the beginning
Thinking about the end
That neither can exist
we can't comprehend.

Candles

Candle of hope
Candle of love
Candle of inspiration.

Candle of light
Candle of peace
Candle of aspiration.

Candle of dreams
Candle of warmth
Candle of mesmerization.

Candle of birth
Candle of death
Candle of transformation.

Candle of thought
Candle of action
Candle of justification.

Candle in the morning
Candle at night
Candle of the spirit
And the power of its flight!

The Beast

Turn around, li'l Annie
a beast is standing at the door!

Turn around, li'l Annie
a beast is standing at the door!

Standing there in hunger
standing there in greed
standing there in anger
from the demon consumption seed!

Turn around, li'l Annie
a beast is standing at the door!

A banker, a broker, a bondsman
and a thief
reaching out their hands to you
seeking your relief!

A blindman, a beggar, a preacher
and a saint
asking for your wisdom
with dignified restraint!

A merchant, a barber, a mechanic
and a clerk
struggling with the burden
of steadily falling worth!

Turn around, li'l Annie
a beast is standing at the door!

A politician, a salesman, an actor
and a fraud
empty out their cures for you
as though they were gods!

A tenant, a debtor, a consumer
and a grunt
don't suggest a cure to them
they want it all up front!

A farmer, an artisan, a skeptic
and the meek
expressing their frustrations
and why they feel so bleak!

Turn around, li'l Annie
a beast is standing at the door!

A lawyer, a gambler, an athlete
and a rake
not wanting anything
they just want to take!

The weary, the frightened, the indigent
and the sad
like a spectrum of the rainbow
they want you to take a stand!

Turn around, li'l Annie
a beast is standing at the door!

Wrapped in waves of satin lace

wrapped in seams of silk and waste
from the low wage labor lands

Fumed, fogged, and furious!

Singing songs of consumption
wailing tunes of conceit
longing for a future
with a never-ending beat!

Turn around, li'l Annie
a beast is standing at the door!

It smashes at the windows
glass upon the floor
the beast is breathing toxins
it's coming through the door!

It's taking all your pictures
your passport and your pearls
it's cutting up your ribbons
graffiti on your murals!

The beast is all about you
no chance now for escape
so cancel your vacation
and hope that you awaken!

Turn around, li'l Annie
a beast is standing at the door!

The Final Exit

Saw her out my window
saw her like a dream
shining like an angel
it was a feeling so supreme

Thought I heard her singing
dancing toward the moon
thought I saw her smiling
gliding toward my room

She moved with grace and freedom
electric was her glow
cascading in the night
like ephemeral summer snow

Thought I saw her coming
running in the night
her hair was flowing wildly
her eyes were shining bright
and then she sat beside me
as if to tempt me more
she said
    'tis not the living I neglect
    it's the passion I ignore
and just as quickly
she flew out the door

The images went crashing
slashing in the air
with danger in the darkness
I could only stare

Thought I heard her crying
thought I saw her dying
reaching out so close to me
but I could only watch futilely

Saw her out my window
fading like a dream
the wind was blowing like a toll
with the passion in her soul

The End of Love

You were the end of love
like a bushel of fallen apples
on the parched ground of my youth
in rapture context taken in full view
embraced by spacious minds
the leaves did fall on my tarnished crown
and before the grandeur of the moment
seized upon the shores of pure delight
so shattered now in passing.

You were the end of love
so quickly gained
so suddenly lost
impervious to the mind, it seemed
but understood at once
the clashing of desire
against the will
of reason against hope
and unadulterated passion fell
like pearls of light adorned from above
extinguished now with falling.

You were the end of love
the last embrace
the final words
your silhouette fading
so etched in memory still
like a mark upon my brow
castles on the sand
waves upon the shore
the promise of the future
gone and never more.

A Persistent Refrain

Across the room, an empty dawn
darkness still upon the floor
waking dreams, I can't ignore
like an enfilading canon roar
raging now within full view
I shift my weight and think of you.

Birds cry at the window sill
cacophony in my ears
a shadow looming in the mirror
bring forth the awful fear
of passion felt so true
the memory lingers still
and I remember you.

The Last Time

Gray as a winter day
without you.
Cold like a night
in December.
Come to my room
like an angel
soon before dawn
through the window
the sweetness sings
the rapture rings
the flight of wings
and you are gone.

Into the Chaos

The cowboy has arrived in town
the autumn leaves are tumbling down
a sassy face is on the clown
I should depart from here!

Wounded politicians play
a futile horn with nothing to say
branded in my mind, they preach
a vapor cloud into the breach
don't believe it's my fault this time!

Through the rain, the Golden Gate
see her eyes in every face
patience glares behind the wait
trumpets blare, but it's too late
to catch the last train!

I tread across the broken street
beggars hide in full retreat
thieves step back with rapid feet
children run and fathers sleep
I reach for them!

But they are gone into the night
and I am lost in bitter strife
the million tongues of threatened life
the air explodes like dynamite
obsessive beasts within the fight
right is wrong, and wrong is right
I reek from it!

A tattooed man on the corner stares
with open arms, he suddenly bares
a voice so quiet in the air
those who seek should always dare
to change the skin they wear
I seek the truth!

The ocean roars a mighty blast
smashing through the struggle cast
wiping out the lurid path
tearing at the beastly past
the human spirit is aghast
the surf is swift
time is fast
I run to it!

The Threshold

The distant rumble of the wind
years and years of struggle past
beckons forth the stubborn change
resistance in my path

The ringing cry is swallowed fast
the loss of youth is in the grass
no more, she sighs
no more at last
but still resistance in my path

I search for truth
it hammers back
the siren's song so incomplete
stampeding in the darkness, wrath
I reach for her in vain, alas
no more, I wail
no more at last

The empty hand
the vacant space
the river will not fill
I cannot take
the dreams of life
from this bitter place

The garden gates are open wide
the greenway slides into the space
before my eyes, the future waits
I must go now
before it's too late
there is no sense in mourning

The life I knew is in the past
the sinful seasons will not last
the tired aims of old have withered dry
I give it up
I say goodbye!

Love Was Just Not Enough

I saw you there in the early morning air
I saw you there and had to stop and stare
It was so sudden to my feeling

It wasn't the moment that caught me so strong
It wasn't the moment that didn't last long
It was the ending that kept me reeling

I got caught in the fog of trying to love you
Afraid I would lose you but couldn't excuse you
Love was just not enough

Even with the good things past
There wasn't enough time to make them last
Words were strong and sometimes rough
The time away was always tough
It always seemed to be tomorrow

The days are long; the years are short
Plans are made, but then you abort
Could have been different, I suppose
But that's the way it always goes
Living life on time you borrow

I got caught in the fog of trying to love you
Afraid I would lose you but couldn't excuse you
Love was just not enough

You say I wasn't there; I say you didn't care
When you were gone and had to think
It wasn't easy to see you sink
It filled my heart with sorrow

Early morning trumpet blares
Restless feet upon the stairs
Sounds so good; you're finally there
But it won't last; it's just not fair
To live my life for tomorrow

I got caught in the fog of trying to love you
Afraid I would lose you but couldn't excuse you
Love was just not enough
Love was just not enough

Now you've gone away
Gone away to stay
Now you've gone away
And I'm okay
I'm okay
I'm okay

China at the End of the Cultural Revolution

Into China

Shanghai came into the darkness
framed within the silhouettes
of scattered lights that gave
the appearance of a densely
populated countryside and
not the largest city in the world.

It came upon us like a dream
surrealistically and somnolently
strange beyond our knowledge
and experience passing beneath
the roaring wings of our arrival.

We bound down the steps like
dignitaries on a secret mission
within the stale, cold silence of
diesel fumes, I felt the stares of
men in green coats and green caps
with red stars above the bill.

My god, the Red Army! I thought.
China!
Mao Tse-tung!
The Long March!
Revolution!

Shanghai

Shanghai in the morning
was like awakening from a pleasant dream
and finding it real and all around you.

Over the railing of the old Imperial Hotel
was a thrilling sight of many people
earnestly engaged in morning exercises
along the waterfront of the vast harbor.

Along the city streets were masses of proletariat
the builders of a new economic order and the
moral and physical strength of New China.

We traversed the old demarcation line between
the historic French and English sectors.
Imagine having your city divided between foreign powers!
Imagine having your country devoured by imperialistic dogs!
The Chinese remember well.
They struggled against it
and won.

Their triumph shined brilliantly in each passing past
their lives rising together in harmony
with production and distribution.
It showed in their social order and responsibility.

Industrial capability became obvious
but it was carefully tailored to the
economic, social, and political needs of the people.

They were too alive with total consciousness
to waste their strenuous efforts on
selfishness and discord.

Thus, working together with a full view of the future
they have reaped the fruits of their labor.
Even the most severe critic could not help but be impressed.

Peng Pu Commune

Peng Pu in the afternoon
brought the reality of communal China
into my brain
seeming like coming home to a way of life
previously only dreamed of and
creating this desire to stay there and
join in the labor of agricultural production.

Greenhouses with growing lush vegetables
in the middle of winter and
sheds with hogs and cows carefully tended
and fields with canal mud being worked in
as fertilizer were only appetizers to the
main course of learning how it all worked
and fit together in the socialist scheme of
teams and brigades of families and their land
of production decisions coordinated with
the national and local agricultural needs.

The people were so involved
and in complete control of all phases of
their lives and their relationship with
production that the insanity of
selfishness and individualism seemed
as outmoded as the feudal system that
darkened their world for so many centuries.

Here was the future at hand, and
clearly visible for scrutiny
it was blushing with the vibrancy
of health and the full, bright color of
the people's faces

they did not quarrel with their mortality
they acted in spite of it within the very
nowness of time to create a society
where people could live up to their potential and
not simply to exist pointlessly.

Their choices in life were meaningful and honed
with clear, sharp edges to be debated and
criticized by all with the purpose of moving
everyone forward at the expense of selfish interests
their freedom became clear and uncluttered
with the narrowness of individuality and
unfettered by the chains of capitalism
the scourge of mankind!

What a fresh breath of air it was, indeed!

Into the Hinterland and the Yellow River

Sound off the rails came rhythmically, chanting
China! China! China!
Sound came pulsating in the cold, still January night
deep into Henan province.
China! China! China!

The vigilance of the Dragon King on earth
sang revolution at each passing station
tucked away in the dead of the cold China night
brightly lit and enamored with the roll
of the earth whose time knows no sleeping.

Racing into the Chinese interior
the sounds of stations passing in the night
like a dream that filled the berth serenely
with the strength of revolutionary change
that glowed through the dark cold
warming the bed of our trekking.

Friendships secured those narrow aisles
and ebbed with yawning smiles.
Awareness grew and passed into awe
that sang off the clicking rails.
China! China! China!

The movement slowed and stopped
winter silence descended
and a station platform stood empty
in the middle of the night along the Yellow River.
Eyes peered out

my eyes
and they gazed searchingly
with fascination and excitement.
China!
Yes!

Heat passed through the train and produced steam
that crept out slowly onto the platform.
A voice over the loudspeaker brought the
enigmatic sounds of China
crashing into my head.
A passing train suddenly broke the silence
with a startling friendly roar
harboring the sounds of socialist accumulation.

China was here all around me
and sleep seemed irreverent
in the snoozing berth of my companions.

Lin County Town

The children played along the street
securely in the evening
within the air, so crisp and sharp
that echoes of China reverberated
through our minds with peace and
tranquility that stirred our souls.

The children ran along the street
laughing and yelling uninhibited
Chinese sounds of youthful gaiety
that carried through the air all of the
strength and wholesomeness
of communal life.

We sat
Country and I
and watched them
and right away, they noticed us as foreigners
in their little town and whooped and hollered
their Chinese greeting and
we played with them the only way we knew how
and they responded, mimicking us when we laughed
and they ran, clapped, and made us full
reducing the gap between our worlds
to a single shred.

A couple passed in eager verse
and others came, carrying and dragging
their tools of socialist production.
A tractor roared down the street
and a truck passed with a blaring horn
and then the streets grew quiet

in the muffled, languid silence
of day's end.

We walked
Country and I
exploring, probing, peeking, and learning
filling our eyes and minds with China
feeling a fullness and freedom never known before.

We met eager faces and shared with them
all that we could
and they responded with all of the
solidarity of international proletarian friendship.

We found language to be no great barrier
and we gave from the depths of our being
and received ecstasy!

It was that kind of a night
when the moon beamed full
and the air breathed radiance
in Lin County, China.

Anyang

It was that night in Anyang
after we have bussed down from
Lin County
when Country and I were waiting
for the room to heat

We were looking at each other
with the same sparkle of the
growing awareness that we were
having one hell of an experience

The steam register hissed
but never grew hot, and we laughed
because our bedrooms at home
were never heated

We knew we could accept this
standard of living, though by
American standards, it was austere
the spirit of the people we had met
had grown into us and
their harmony of effort gave us
a desire to join them

For what greater purpose could be given
than the construction of a society where
basic needs were worked on first
when there was a sense of purpose
in every encounter

How could we not help but glow inside
with this fine reinforcement of our dedication.

Wang Su Chia Brigade

There was trust in the room
emanating from the faces
and the manners of our hosts
that was becoming pleasantly familiar

It was the way the young people
sat at the end of the table, eating the peanuts
that were piled in front of them and
so graciously offered to us
with bowls of sweet potatoes
and tea and cigarettes

The brigade was obviously materially poor
but rich with selflessness, sharing, and
communal spirit

There was a decisive enjoyment of life
expressed at the end of the table
for, though the quantitative accomplishments
of their endeavors were meager
it was the fruit of their labor that shined
and it was growing every year, and
they were pleased to share it with us

The cold air sifted beneath
the rug-covered doorway
but the warmth of the food
and the smiles of the young people
heated the room with a most pleasant
and satisfying feeling of oneness
streaking through my bones.

Tiger Head Hill

I sat on Tiger Head Hill, looking down on Tachi
across the narrow ravine to my left stood
members of the PLA, dutifully listening to the
proud accomplishments of this tiny brigade.
They were looking at the old caves, where the people
once lived in, left there as a reminder of their hard past
when three landlords controlled everything, and
peasants sold their children to have money to buy food
after the floods rushed down from the hills and ruined
their fields and homes.

To my right, a small group of children came frolicking
down the winding hill road from the mountains, and
I couldn't quite hear them, but my senses detected
an unrestrained merriment that left sounds of
freedom in my ears that came hopping and skipping
to the beat of New China.

On the opposite hillside, a goat herder was ambling
about the small herd
a shepherd of the communal flock
raised there with socialist production
that transformed their lives from deep poverty
to the fulfillment of basic needs.

The crisp, warm air of that unusual January day
when the sun was bright and the sky was clear
felt like home in Western Kansas
halfway around the rolling earth
and it brought to me a new awareness
of a discovery of a state of mind I had been searching for
created in the atmosphere of China.

It was as clear and lucid as the view before me
on Tiger Head Hill.

China had permeated my being
my legs were sending runners into the soil
the air seemed rare and intoxicating
with a freedom of senses that I had never experienced
and it was exhilarating to feel its strength.

It passed too soon
and I suddenly felt detached
as though I were looking at Tachi
through a window display case
and I recognized that my life
was not here, but in the madness
of the capitalist world.
It was a sobering effect, and
I struggled with it until Tachi
was only a memory.

The Chinese Woman

She captured my heart with just a smile
her beauty revealed an inner spirit of
unexploited striving
caused no sexual stimulation
as much as I tried
made me feel complete
and yearn for revolution.

Bundled up in her layers of clothing
she didn't need perfume or lotion
or fancy hair or
revealing curves
or long lashes
her inner spirit revealed her beauty.

Her presence brought no fear
no fantasy
only a singular, strong desire
to struggle together
she needs no bed to win her man
no sweet cooing
no promises
she uses consciousness and theory
wrapped together in practice
how I appreciated her!

It is capitalism that exploits and
suppresses American women and my woman
and myself
causes us to reach for superficialities
and lustful manipulations
Madison Avenue has cajoled us into

accepting this as reality and
we haven't struggled against it
nearly enough!

Unraveling the Myth

Gaping through the bus window
somewhere along the China trail
we were blazing
I became aware of something
from the childhood years
when I believed everything I was told
about my country, the United States of America.

It's strange, the way those words
can still sound good and send a
shiver up my spine amidst the awareness
of how twisted my country has become
and the confused way in which it
collectively thinks.

The United States of America!

Wasn't that where the people had
so much to say about their lives
about their government
about everything?

Wasn't that where people were freer
than any other people on the face of the earth
where everyone had a good heart and
the policeman was your best friend?

Wasn't that where the bastion of freedom
and democracy rested
the great defender of world peace and freedom?

Wasn't that where the people had all the good
things in life and never suffered from any wants?

The United States of America!

Wasn't that where you grew old like a tree
and could be just as stable and beautiful?

Wasn't that where everyone in the world
yearned to be and struggled for in the
tyrannies of the world?
Wasn't That the Absolute Truth?
I certainly believed it to be so
until, that is, I grew older and faced
the realities of life and, in time, slipped
into the oblivion of alienation and severe want
which forced thoughts of another life
that would truly conform to the earlier beliefs
which people in an amazing contradiction
would always say was pure utopian idealism.

So then, it can be understood why it was so
startling to be gazing out a bus window
in the middle of China somewhere and realize
all those beliefs had finally found a home.

Chu Ping Ho

When I first saw Chu standing there
smiling broadly and shaking everyone's hand
I feared he was a communist Uncle Tom
but he was solid
theoretically correct
worthy of the title, comrade.

His layers of cotton clothing were thick
enough to play football, tall with a small
birthmark setting off his cheekbone
he was a Nanking, family man, and teacher.

He was the corridor walker in the morning
"Bentlee," "Flora," I can still hear him
ringing in his proper English accent
"Time to get a move on"
"Let's get moving."

When questions were asked, reeking of lingering
McCarthy induced fear and the conviction that
America was God's gift to civilization
Chu played marvelously dumb and would ask
With a wrinkled brow and serious eyes
"What was that again?"
I couldn't blame him.

He was the bearer of sad news and openly
wept in grief when Chou En-lai passed away.
America had so few leaders worthy of tears.

Toward the end of the trip, he began to withdraw
and I wasn't sure why, although

he may have been tired of us
and the frequent, though largely unintended
belittling of his people and their accomplishments.
Possibly he had grown fond of us
and was merely preparing himself
emotionally for our departure.

Sentiment has no place in revolution
and though people come and go
revolutionaries remain forever.

New China

Everyone agreed
the Chinese people sure did work hard
indeed!

What some of our fellow travelers
couldn't understand was why?
They wanted to see slave gangs
and guards with guns and dogs
and physical coercion
but what they saw, they didn't want to believe.
People working together without a profit motive
with no incentive of personal reward
and self-advancement, nor plush living
or large bank rolls.

It was really quite simple
the Chinese people worked hard because they wanted to
because there was a reason, a purpose for
the construction of a socialist society
without exploited labor, where
all could share the benefits according to their needs.

They had a work ethic where all contribute
according to their ability
because labor is the source of wealth
and capital accumulation
something China has always lacked.
The Chinese know this and believe
their labor will result in a better life
for everyone, not just a few.

And because of this, they cared for each other
unbelievably with genuine concern
if one worker slacked, they were all hurt
thus, great pressure was exerted on each person
to work as hard as they could, and
marching together, they are moving
toward a new society.

Norman Bethune

When I first heard the story of Pai Chu-En
I was angry because he hadn't taken better
care of himself
but later, when I discovered about
the way he lived and the way he died
I felt only the greatest admiration
and inspiration.

He was an artist, inventor, scholar, teacher
soldier, doctor, and a student
full of passion, energy, and love of life
and foremost, a revolutionary of the highest order.

His life was woven with courage and dedication to people
and he made a tempest of the struggle to give life
and he gave fully and completely.

He hated tyranny with a rage barely under control
and when he gave his life
he left a monument
that caused tyranny to shudder.

White-Seek-Grace
Pai Chu-En
A mountain leveled in the sun.

Sid Engst

They thought he was one of us
but he wasn't.

They thought he would give us
the real scoop
the inside story
the real truth for a change
and he did
but it wasn't what they wanted to hear.

He spoke softly with firm assurance
that disarmed his listeners
and he talked of the New China
with a quiet pride.
China is his life now
and you could feel the strength
it gave him
the strength we had felt everywhere
of inner peace, security, and belief
in struggle as the cutting edge.

They thought he was one of us
but he wasn't
he was a revolutionary.

Tiananmen Square

Walking along the broad, modern
Chang'an Boulevard, the next to last night in China
on my way to pay respects to Chou En-lai
at the Monument to the People's Heroes
in the middle of the massive Tiananmen Square
with the fierce Peking wind pounding into my face
burning the Chinese cigarette I was smoking
into my black leather gloves
it was a time to reflect on a strange peace of mind
that was telling me I wanted to stay in China
and become Chinese so I could participate
in what seemed like a pure agrarian democracy
adjusted to the needs of the hundreds of millions of peasants.

The evening had turned into night
with bicycles in pairs, singles, and triplets
gliding quietly down the avenue as
the riders were bending their heads
against the wind and crocking them toward me.
Bicycles were everywhere in China with
a few motorized scooters but no automobiles
which were solely reserved for government officials.

I crossed the boulevard toward the monument
which stood opposite the Forbidden Palace
where Mao resided in his last year of life.
The monument was covered, and the space
around it was filled with hundreds of
artificial flower wreath arrangements
that groups of people had been seen for

several days bringing them in pilgrimages
to pay tribute to Chou.

I stood there for a while, thinking about the
trip and everything we had seen
and of the role Mao and Chou had played in it
considering myself to be a Maoist
being aware of the harsh things the West
said about him, calling him a tyrant and
murderer in the same league as Hitler and Stalin
but believing it was an unfair and inaccurate
characterization of him, considering all of the
good things he had done and the massive
upheaval of accumulated millenniums of
oppression and poverty, he had overturned.
Chou, in a way, seemed more respected by
everyone, including the Chinese, but, to them,
Mao was a god.

I concluded that night that the West
could never understand the Chinese, and
the revolutionary changes and what they meant
to the Chinese without being here to actually
see what was happening and put that
into the context of history.

At least for a while, I thought I understood
and felt at one with them.

Reflections

They said we had been duped.
They said we had been fooled.
They said we were naive and too idealistic, and
these were the liberals among us
who knew nothing about Chinese history
and the struggle of its people
over more than two millenniums
but everyone was interested, and
it was an opportunity to discuss and
inform our friends and neighbors
even if they didn't totally believe us.

China was a world unto itself
with a billion people being released
from bondage after a long period of
isolation, feudalism, and poverty.

It was impossible to form a consensus
among such a huge population
as to what was happening
in their emerging country.
The bourgeois classes and intellectuals
hated the Cultural Revolution because
it forced them to interact with the peasants
and rural population, so there could be
a better understanding and appreciation
of their struggle, cultural contributions
and technological needs.
The peasants and rural people were
emboldened in ways they had never
experienced to control their own lives

by suppressing the warlords, the landlords
and the waterlords.

The revolution we witnessed in China
would not last much longer.
Capitalism gained ascendancy and did
great things for the few, but left behind the many.
What we experienced was perhaps only a chapter
in a revolution that will be continued in the future.

Fanshen!

The Kalalau Trail

The Kalalau Trail

Kalalau rises quickly beneath the heathen feet
pulling like a magnet buried in the rock
drawing the fearless through a dark unknown
into an uncommon reality
full of peril, challenge, and rapture.

The path is shrouded in darkness
of a never-known sun
lined with slabs of flat black rocks
intermeshed with potholes and boulders
large and small
a slippery, hardened turf
rising above Kee Beach
a sacred place of awe and power.

From the ashes of blessed spirits
by unknown gods
and soil from the deep forbidden zone of the earth
the armed combatants flail upon the ocean
smashing the terra firma with eternal commitment
and all the radiance of the shining heavens falls upon it!

There in the distance
through a gap in the foliage
brightened by the sun into being
yonder doth godly Odysseus ride
in all his plumed glory
flaming through the fields
behind winged white stallions
with Menelaus and Patroclus at his sides
fairly flying through the screaming air
and trailing pure vapor streams

from the eye of the storm
at the edge of all that can be known
into eternity!

Kalalau rises beneath our feet
so carefully placed between the cracks and crevices
around loose rocks, tumbling with just a touch
and always gripping upward
to four hundred feet in a quarter of a mile
the fury rages on the ocean floor
now cresting with a perfect view
soon to be left behind.

The Kalalau Trail winds in and around
and up and down the Na Pali Coast
like a piece of silk slipped around the curvature
of the Great Mother
neatly tugging at the feet
light cool air breezing from the crests
across the dampened brow
soon boiling in the sun
behind a newly found resolve.

We pause in the cool, light air
and gape in wonder
before trekking onward toward Hanakapiai Valley
a mile and a half distant
over the rocky, red clay path
atop a mountain that is only
a foothill to greater crags.

The air is clean and fragrant
and the sun is bright and gaining heat
in the midmorning.

Firm, long, slender, and serrated
yucca plant leaves
crowd the path along the way
and brush against our bare legs
but doesn't scratch.

Spindly pineapple trees
rise from multi-pod roots
above the course ground
like a tree on a platform.

Plant life not identified
teems at every turn
but wildlife is scarce
to the beholden.

An overly sweet
fruity scent that robs the air of freshness
pushes us around the crest
into a narrow valley and around another crest
into a broader valley
ascending
descending
winding back and forth across the mountaintop
deeper along the coast
lined with rough, rocky mountains
stretching higher and higher into the brilliant sky.

Hanakapiai looms beneath us
with an even fresher breath of air
churned by multiple layers of violent surf
crashing into a beach of large, black
round volcanic rocks and boulders
replaced by a green wave of pineapple trees and plant life
and split down the middle of the valley
by a sparkling river, flowing over and around the boulders.

Not to drink the water, we are warned
or else the dread sickness will descend
danger lurking within the blessing
evil in the heart of good
spurs the mind to contemplation
of all the contraries
and unifications that occur within our midst
creating an order that is largely untouched by man.

Kalalau beckons us further
like a temptress from the wild.

    Walk upon my soil!
    Tramp along my narrow path!
    Treat yourself to my mysteries
    revealed before your eager eyes
    so long lost from seeing!

Hanakapiai Beach sinks beneath our feet
as Kalalau rises through a series of switchbacks
on a wide, sticky, red path
that is drying as we walk.

Quickly, we climb two hundred feet
and then another hundred
back and forth
leaving Hanakapiai far below
and then it disappears
as we continue to rise
on a parallel path across the face of a mountain.

Hearts beat double time
lungs explode with heaving bursts
feet move steadily with sureness in their stepping
as the path narrows to a width no greater
than a cow path in Dad's south pasture.

Grass and yucca plants cover the trail
and we rise higher above the ocean
curling in and around the edge of the mountains
like seekers of lost memories.

At the Gate, we reach 1,200 feet
but it feels like 2,000
at the threshold of heaven
high above the surf
between the mountain and a huge boulder
on the edge of the precipice
where a wind gusts through the passage
and wild boars are barred from entry
into a wide, high valley
entombed with green life
and tropical heat seared
by the midday sun.

Switchbacks descend
embedded in the thin red soil
and curl into the center of the valley
weaving the web of life itself
delivering unto the ebb and flow
the being and doing
of conscious reflection
and perturbation
of twists and turns
and unexpected reality
with avowals of memory and appreciation
up and down
in and around
churning
relaxing
steadily grinding the will
into a passion blessed with seeing
stirring the mind

flaming the soul
hardening the body
with uneven passing
and driving resolve
for the relentless quest
Hanakoa!

Hanakoa in the midday sun
wrapped in a maze of tropical life
and internal upheavals
enduring and saturated with the eternal plan
so distant from the artificial design
only touched by its brief passing
quickly absorbed with more powerful rhythms
into the tangled watershed
entreating with wild goats
finger falls and squalid heat.

Returning thus to where we came
we must
resolve again with a further burst
to reap the fullness of that resolve
from the opposite side of being
from timelessness to life
beyond good and evil
into the spiritual kingdom
of our deliverance!

Passing
passing
we are always passing
from what we were into
what we become
and for the moment only
in the brief glimmer
of the sparkling life

so cleansed from paltry seeking
doth the breath of our coming
discover the presence of our being!

O great, glorious sun
shine down upon me radiantly
shed me from the past
and bring me peace!

About the Author

Mr. Bentley is a native of the sprawling grasslands of Gove County, along the Smokey Hill River in Western Kansas. He is a graduate of Kansas State University and Washburn University Law School. After law school, he managed a land title business and practiced law in Jackson County, Kansas. In 1980, he organized the Kansas Rural Center as an advocacy organization in support of organic farming, alternative energy, resource conservation, family farms, and rural communities. Mr. Bentley became the director of affordable housing finance and development for the State of Kansas in 1991 and held that position until 2020. He currently resides in Manhattan, Kansas.